McGRAW-HILL ADVANCED SERIES IN ECONOMICS

Consulting Editor
N. Gregory Mankiw

Economic Growth
 by Robert J. Barro and Xavier Sala-i-Martin

Advanced Macroeconomics
 by David Romer

ADVANCED
MACROECONOMICS

ADVANCED MACROECONOMICS

David Romer
University of California, Berkeley

The McGraw-Hill Companies, Inc.
New York   St. Louis   San Francisco   Auckland   Bogotá   Caracas
Lisbon   London   Madrid   Mexico City   Milan   Montreal   New Delhi
San Juan   Singapore   Sydney   Tokyo   Toronto

This book was set in Lucida Bright by Publication Services, Inc.
The editor was Lucille Sutton;
the production supervisor was Friederich W. Schulte.
The cover was designed by Delgado Design;
the cover illustration was drawn by Shane Kelley.
Project supervision was done by Publication Services, Inc.
R. R. Donnelley & Sons Company was printer and binder.

McGraw-Hill

A Division of The **McGraw·Hill** *Companies*

ADVANCED MACROECONOMICS

This book is printed on acid-free paper.

1A 2 3 4 5 6 7 8 9 0 DOC DOC 9 0 9 8 7 6 5

ISBN 0-07-053667-8

Library of Congress Cataloging-in-Publication Data

Romer, David.
    Advanced macroeconomics / David Romer.
       p. cm. — (McGraw-Hill advanced series in economics)
    Includes bibliographical references and index.
    ISBN 0-07-053667-8
    1. Macroeconomics.   I. Title.   II. Series.
  HB172.5.R66   1996
   339—dc20   95-37228

ABOUT THE AUTHOR

David Romer is professor of economics at the University of California, Berkeley. He received his A.B. from Princeton University, where he was valedictorian, and his Ph.D. from M.I.T. He has been on the faculty at Princeton and has been a visiting faculty member at M.I.T. and Stanford. He is also a Research Associate of the National Bureau of Economic Research and serves on the editorial boards of several economics journals. His main research interests are monetary policy, the foundations of price stickiness, empirical evidence on economic growth, and asset-price volatility. He is married to Christina Romer, who is also an economist, and has two children, Katherine and Paul.

To Christy

CONTENTS IN BRIEF

CONTENTS IN BRIEF